W0115373

SWEAR
HAKIM
BELLAMY

Cover & author photos:
Mikhayla Harrell
Book design: Adam Rubinstein

Printed in the United States
of America

First print edition April 2013
ISBN 97809826968-9-7

West End Press
P.O. Box 27334
Albuquerque, NM 87125

For book information, see our
website at www.westendpress.org

PUBLICATION CREDITS

Citizens United
Truthout, Democratic Party of Chavez County, Occupy New Mexico, Democracy for New Mexico

I'm in love with a 1%er
Politicomments.com, El Grito, The Occupy Wall Street Poetry Anthology, Democracy for New Mexico

The Pits
Commissioned for Anti-Racism Day 2012, delivered at the NM State Legislature Roundhouse Rotunda

Literacy Test
(AKA The New Jim Crow)
Counterpunch, Más Tequila Review

The Art of War
NM CultureNet/Santa Fe Community College Poetry Matters Video

Children of the Sunday
200 New Mexico Poems

Silent Sanctuary
Zingara Poet, excerpted in Double Tongue (broadside)

PERFORMANCE CREDITS

Different Classrooms
Excerpt of talk for TEDxABQ. Used as audio in the closing credits of 2010 New Mexico Solutions Gap Summit video by the State of NM

Silent Sanctuary
Written in response to a composition by Kathleen Ryan for Double Tongue, sponsored by NM Humanities Council.

Letter to Hip Hop I
Urban Verbs, Barelas, ABQ, USA 06.17.2011

Letter to Hip Hop II
Urban Verbs, Barelas, ABQ, USA 06.18.2011

Letter to Hip Hop II
Urban Verbs, Barelas, ABQ, USA 06.19.2011

CITIZENS UNITED

WORK

LETTER TO HIP HOP

CITIZENS UNITED

CITIZENS UNITED

ON THE RECENT ELECTIONS

I

If we kidnapped
their children
they would find us
if we put guns
in the hands of those young
they would tag them
"child soldiers"
instead
we let them steal them
leave them clinically depressed
decorate them in marine

there is a name
for people who will take
the very bread
off of our dinner table
and put it in their pocket
they are toast
like champagne flutes
are the new silver spoon
like what they will be
when the revolutions
and the riots
catch up with them

tomorrow morning
when humanity
has the munchies

and eats presidential candidates
for breakfast
when their war chest
can fill the holes
in our country's
debt, deficit & addiction
and they'd rather
raise money
to argue about it
than raise sleeves
to fix it

II

politicians are not people too, Mitt
look at you!
and they're not Jesus either, Barack
if you remember
he ran the moneychangers out of the temple
not into his cabinet
if you remember
he was Guantanamo's blueprint
if you remember
he did not run for office
he ran for his life
he was no popularity contestant
he had no friend in the Pharaoh, Pharisees or FED
he told them
where they could shove
their opinion poll
and they hung him from it
back in the day

when Romans lynched Jews
with perpendicular sticks
you remember
they make sure you do
'cause from the dome of the United States Capitol
to the Pantheon bars of the White House
boy, they gon' make sure that you know
where Black people are supposed to live
if you remember
he did not run for office
he ran for his life

whatever happened
to public servants?
instead of self-serving
when did it stop
being about "We the People"
    and start
being about winning?
when did the Catholic's
social doctrine
and the atheist's
social justice
both translate to
"go to hell?"
why do we wait for them?
for education
for elections
then wonder
why we won't teach us
to elect ourselves
what if

every lawn's
campaign sign
read "Peace"
what if
on November 6th
we'd agree
          to agree
what if
I were to say
I'll only believe
in a government
that believes
in me
what if the citizens
were really united
and each one of us
individually decided
"I'll vote for me."

I'M IN LOVE WITH A 1%ER

FOR OCCUPY WALL STREET

I should have been alarmed
when you started speaking in equations
numerical manipulations
and your stories didn't add up

human expression cost too much
so you began sending me
bank statements instead of love letters

you,
the one I trusted with my parents' retirement
and my children's future
promised to be there when I needed you
that we were in this together
then bailed

with every red cent
I worked so hard for
to keep you in the black

I should have known
you would bleed me for everything I own
when our conversations
became computations
before you stopped speaking to me at all

you looked at me differently
I was the first customer of your mom and pop's shop
    you were dowered in store credit
carded

'cause you looked too young to qualify
for your first small business loan
you loved government assistance then
and only love socialism for the rich now

your eyes glinted like a castrated bull
you began seeing me
flush with rouge and sweat and stress
I was your employee then
did what was best for "the team"
took the pay cuts
gave the benefits up
because what was good for you
was good for "Us"

you traveled
left me home
with kids and student loans
to man your phones
while you said

"Baby, I'm only gon' be gone for a few months.
Once we get these factories stacked up, I'll send for you.
I'm doing this for us."

Soon you had more employees there
than here
younger and cheaper than me
barely legal
for you and your off shore whores

the last time I saw you
you did not see me
you crept into our apartment
at 18 Broad Street
to grab your accounting
take it back to your island bank
without so much as kissing me on the forehead
son and daughter laying in bed beside me
you didn't even kiss your futures goodbye

because you didn't want to wake them
but now they are awake
screaming for you
to leave
you look at me differently now
like an obstacle
like you could have been more
without taking care of my freeloading ass
like you could have had more
without overpaying wages to my lazy ass
like you could have made more
without the rules
without thinking about other people besides yourself
without me nagging you about human rights
environmental protections
and genocide

you made more shit
than we could possibly need
more than we could possibly greed
when you ran out of a middle class to feed
you were made paranoid by your dogs eating each other

and made the competition
me

I should have seen it coming
when we began breaking dishes and bedroom doors
over which Presidential Candidates we'd support
you wanted the ones you could buy
I wanted the ones I voted for
you began acquiring houses
by selling them to people you knew couldn't afford them
you picked up a gambling problem
kept lying about some shit
that didn't exist on the stock market
then one day you got drunk on your own stories
told so many lies you forgot where they started
almost got stung
ended up buying your own junk
bonded out of jail just in time to OD our economy
put that stuff so deep in your vanity
our hopes and dreams
collapsed with your arteries

but there's always a silver lining
silver I'll never put in your possession again
I was in an abusive relationship with a bankster
    before you
but because I promised myself that never again
would I believe anything a junkie says
'cause I seen you selling since
new car, new suit, new parachute,
looking like a bonus

yo ass could almost pass for a man, but I know:
if there's one thing I learned

seeing the entire financial industry on its knees
begging for a piece of my tax dollars
like it would save their lives
flatlined on the floor of 11 Wall St.
black three piece suit,
not a drop of blood
after being shot in the head twice

still alive
while my hands
cup my insides
as the floor of my country floods
with all ten pints of me.
if there's one thing I learned

it's that corporations aren't people
because people die
in the streets.

LIQUID

Margins
have always been better for profit
than for the people that live there

where lower class
looks like an accomplishment
from down here

where the ups
and the Dows
of the Joneses

feel more like
the down
and the outs of the Jeffersons
no Black laundromat
to wash the slavery off legal tender

no dirty employers
blaming second generation dreamers
for their money not
being clean

our very survival
is a roller coaster
with highs
and lows
that make market fluctuations
look as eventful as
a puddle of blood.

we may not make the business segment
of the nightly news
but if you study the income gap graph
intently enough
as it crawls comatose
across the heart rate monitor
of the TV screen
look closely in between
and you can read

"Police line do not cross"
on this block of Wall Street
where people were auctioned alive
for profit
there's a crime scene
in chalk
the same color as the school bus
children disembark
to labor an outline
the shape of a ship

we are victims here

slavery is not dead
the first wave of economics
bought us across
the middle class-age

spreading the doctrine
of self-consumption
like a crusade
making savages of saints

surplus of security
substance

America
off-shoring our sweat-shopped dream
to countries
no more likely
to buy our exports
than our bullshit

we know it's bull
and bear, these markets
like the corporate class
hasn't farmed free labor
into the DNA of our country
by the corpseload

we're dying for growth
in an economic system
that suffocates us with success
'cause competition knows best
and we won't be happy
til there's no one else left

our math is all wrong
numbers
without the lives attached to them
can't be counted on
fingers and toes
a pregnancy with complications
denied bedside pre-natal
'cause our healthcare is attached to our paychecks

not to our home
of the brave
brave enough to tell our elders
to pull the plug
tell our young
"Shut the fuck up!
'Cause you ain't old enough
to use four letter words like…"
inflation

way too young
to contribute to the GDP
and that's a God Damn Problem
America has an "I Don't Care" economy
where we're either under the table
or under the bus
even under the water

America will get the wall it has always wanted
when bodies start filling the Rio Grande up

12,000 stories high
taller than the banks in Manhattan
sitting on 1.7 Trillion
of liquid
while a country burns around us

golden parachutes packed
in case we make it to the corner office
unlikely, but not unheard of
even London is burning right now

the rich will jump
take this entire slave ship
the whole corporation-caboodle
down with them
rewarded handsomely
for taking that risk
incorporation and bankruptcy are their safety nets

their East Indian Tea Party
drown us in the bath water
because dependents are an expensive
liability

so we stay at the margins
ant farm after ant farm
we cultivate the industrial
average
our standard is poor
we are the property of our employers
held hostage
by a safety net we romanticize

that does not exist

we won't rock the boat
even when they can us in the bottom
like blue fin tuna
even when our children
starve to death
next to us
in a pile of our own feces
even when it's always dark

and someone is always screaming

we are pushed to the edge
didn't jump when we could have
missed the boat
like we'd actually
miss
this
boat

rode a piece of ship to America
convincing ourselves
that one day
it'll be a yacht

made to believe
we can't swim
out here
where the water is free

THE PITS

The unique thing about lies is
they only go backwards in time
a fabrication about the past
can be corroborated
but when you make up
your future
they call it a dream

so would I be lying
if I told you
the Constitution
was cut from
the same cherry tree
George Washington forgot
to lie about?

or would I be sleeping,
and only call the Constitution
a liar
if I were awake?

but we're going to
talk about
dreams today

we're going to pretend
the day you lose
your faith in people
doesn't feel
like a broken heart

a bad day
waiting to happen
so inevitable,
I've marked it on my calendar
already made time
to nurse my son's soul
and eat gallons of salt

his first day of school
the first time someone calls him a …

we're going to dream
that martyrs
don't die for nothing
that people don't go to jail
for the crime
of their skin

that the sound
of a prison door
and a heart unlocking
sound the same

we're going to visualize
the luxury sedan
apple pie man
three-piece suit
on the outside of the vehicle
license and registration in hand

being asked
"How did you make your money?"

"Who did you hurt to get this?"
K-9 sniffing his car
for privilege

we're going to picture
profiling different
picture profiling non-existent

we're going to imagine
a blood money economy
not founded on the backs
of cotton-pickin'
Native, African, Mexican
hyphen-any-American

we're going to imagine
we're gonna John Lennon
we're going to invent
    concepts that don't exist
like "Race"
and erase racism
until we don't have to be
"Anti-" anything

we want concepts like
Love-ism
because I've never seen
people love each other apart
they're usually
loving each other back
together again
we're going to fantasize

the color of my son's skin
pretend it was a nightmare
that states had laws
making it illegal
for two people
to make a miracle
the complexion of Jesus
as brown-olive as Muhammad

we used to think down
but now?

we're gonna think up
a world that would never
dream up legislation
that would stop us
from making love
though we live in one that still does

we're gonna masquerade
in our great-grandmother's star-spangled gown
dress up as the country
we said we'd be
instead of what we were
because a country that lives in black and white
will never be able to dream in color

we're gonna fake it like the cherry tree
that birthed the parchment
that bore the Declaration of Independence
that bore our country
we're gonna pretend

that *that* tree
did not bear strange fruit too

like the Bill of Rights
does not have blood
on
  its
    roots

we're going to pretend
our founding fathers would be crying
at the revelation
that what they wrote in 1776
was fiction
not fact

that the Constitution
is being used
as a short story
not a contract

we're going to dream today
that all men are created equal
and we're gonna pretend
that we hold these truths

to be self-evident.

FIRST, YOU LAUGHED

FIRST THEY IGNORE YOU,
THEN THEY LAUGH AT YOU,
THEN THEY FIGHT YOU,
THEN YOU WIN.
—GANDHI

We couldn't even afford to protest
until you gave up our jobs, America
you wanted us on the streets
now we're home

built elaborate institutions of hired learning
taught us nothing, except
how to go into debt

we're right where you want us
sleeping in the park
next to garbage can
erupting with diplomas
that will finally be worth
their weight in paper and
keep the heat on

the constitution will not be televised
broadcast
or brought to you by Citibank
assembly is a right
not a permit

employed media and fear
to keep us in homes we don't own
in these times

where it takes more paperwork
to congregate
than to segregate

welcome to you, America
home of the Dollar Store
where everything is 99 percent

Land of the Free
(for now)
and for the first six months
but after that
interest is a bitch

gave us banks
instead of better standards of living
where the average worker
puts life, liberty and the pursuit of happiness
on lay-a-way

gave us credit
instead of competitive wages
cheapened our children's education
then said if we want the good shit
we can pay for it

said there's too much overhead
to let us retire
which is about as American
as McDonald's apple pies

made the Statue of Liberty a liar
gave her our tired, our poor
as we're here
huddled en masse yearning to breathe free
in the name of freedom
we're dying in the streets

dying at our desks
noose a life insurance policy around our neck
just to pay the rent
pays out better than health insurance
'cause when we're dead
there's less risk
while premiums are spent
on financial instruments that don't fuckin' exist

orphaned us to a system
that blames us when we die
use the market to hide behind
statements like
"Health care is not a human right."

blame our death on our love of freedom
when the heart attack and hypertension
come from being under attack
every working day of our lives

the bottom line
is not just to separate us
from our money

it is to separate us, from one another
'cause when people get together 'round some bullshit
they'll organize the fuck out of each other

so I won't listen to you tell me that
unions are the problem
and the WTO is here to help
or that "For quality purposes"
you gotta privatize the information
Cadillac plan the Internet
while the bought and sold
corporate media has been for sale

tell me another one
'cause laughter is the only thing
I can afford right now

tell me that job creation
isn't the furthest thing
from the minds of the 1%
'cause you ain't gotta be Noble Prize winner in economics
to know that low wages and labor
equal high profits

tell me another one
like being a patriot means being silent
like Dr. King's legacy wasn't manufactured
into a corporate icon
like he didn't get a bullet in his head
as soon as he started talking about poverty

like he didn't say
"There comes a time when silence is betrayal."

tell me another one
Herman "Fuckin'" Caine
to blame myself
for being 99 and not 1
for being on the losing end of a class war
started by "people"
(in tax designation only)
with their hands so far up your ass
that you Muppet Marie Marionette phrases like
"Let them eat cake."

this is not a laughing matter
we've been out here for months
and winter is coming
our homes don't have heat
and yours do

you've even banned us from the park benches
so guess who coming to dinner?

what used to be a problem of the poor
is now a problem of yours...
there's a Russian Proverb that goes:
"The rich would have to eat money
if the poor did not provide food"
but what do we eat
when we have nothing else to lose
to you.

LITERACY TEST
(AKA THE NEW JIM CROW)

ANY PERSON WHO SHALL ATTEMPT TO TEACH ANY FREE PERSON OF COLOR, OR
SLAVE, TO SPELL, READ OR WRITE, SHALL, UPON CONVICTION THEREOF BY
INDICTMENT, BE FINED IN A SUM NOT LESS THAN TWO HUNDRED FIFTY DOLLARS.
—FROM THE ALABAMA SLAVERY CODE OF 1833

When they can no longer steal our land
they'll steal our books
because every genocide
starts with the mind
every revolution
begins with a thought
and heart

they will sacrifice
our freedom of teach
and only
by the grace of the laws they created
can they not
sacrifice our hearts
to stakes and nooses
bombs, gunfire and arson

but believe me
they've tried

so plan B
is to make us
love ourselves less
if burning women at the stake
couldn't kill feminism

how the hell
they think they gon' ban Chicanismo?

we ain't scared of a state
that will burn and ban people
because we are burnt and banned people
they won't even let us keep
the perfect bound papers we got

these hypocrites
are fittin' to get their history undocumented
displace pen from paper
like people from places
remove Mexican-American hands
from the first Catholic Church ever built
in Solomonville, Arizona
1887

at First Presbyterian Church
in Morenci
1889
remove the pictures
of brown Jesus
who looks more Mexican
than Methodist

remove the Immaculate Heart of Mary Church
we built
because we were tired
of being forced to listen to mass
in the basement of St. Mary's

erase the deportation
of a thousand copper miners
on strike in Bisbee
left on a train car
in the New Mexican desert
by vigilantes
with no food
or water

a government
that so badly wants
the history of how
we "got it"
to be forgotten
they will remove fingerprints
from a crime scene

remove César Chávez's birth
from Yuma

remove César Chávez
Gloria Anzaldúa
Tomás Rivera
Luis Valdez
Martín Espada
Isabel Allende
Rudolfo Anaya
Rodolfo Acuña and Gonzáles
no Elizabeth Martínez
not even in pictures

no Mexican white boys
and no women hollerin' creek
NO! Sherman Alexie

just like Pocahontas and John Smith
Thanksgiving and bullshit
the Lone Ranger and Tonto
will not fist fight in heaven
they will hold hands

no zoot suit
nobody's son
everybody's "Bro"…
no Codexes
only Rolexes
no Black Mesa poems

Arizona
wouldn't even leave
Baldwin and Zinn alone
said, "F.U." to Rosales
Abu-Jamal
and Henry David Thoreau

no rethinking Columbus
no rethinking anything
as a matter of fact
no thinking
period

because the ruling class
will have us drink Kool-aid

instead of cultura
because there is no single act worse
than the revisionist history they hate
than removing books
from schools

I want to tell America
that bleaching the brown
off your history
will not make you clean
that there is no way
to separate your guilt
from truth

that there is
an "X" in la raza II
and just because your history
is unswallowable without milk
and we are like water for chocolate
that's no excuse

so we'll build
a bridge of banned books
'cross the border

and when you find yourself
so far from God
that you need to borrow
that bridge to get back

we won't even ask
for your papers

we'll just open our history books
and keep track
because the only people
that are afraid of the past
are people who are afraid of facts

let me get this straight?
you want to remove books
from our tragically
underperforming education system?
maintaining "It's not about race"
when it's obvious
that it's not about class?

this is a
"You-are-not-allowed-to-have-a-history" lesson
where there are only
closed book tests
because you don't want us
to pass.

DIFFERENT CLASSROOMS

I'm not a teacher but I teach
have taught and still do
but now the classrooms are different

forced back to patient from doctorate
from masters to novice
from professor to scholar
from teacher to college to high school problem, "Child . . .
now the students have the knowledge!"
and we're catching up

I've sat in labs
with 22 separate experiments
conducting experiments
and a few "anti-social" reactions gone wrong
have me wondering what their parents meant

or didn't mean when they had them
but the feeling is mutual
because neither do we get to select the folks that have us
but they have us

and these are the discourses we're not having
sitting here
genetically splitting hairs,
splitting atoms

while I remember taking courses about family matters
home economics
birth control and abstinence
'cause the real world out there

looks nothing like our idealistic theories
and sanitized classrooms
instead of distrusting the "disruptions"
who are fed up with our demagoguery
we shove at them

how can we pretend we're puzzled when
the fact of the matter is
it's disgusting the discussions we're not having
so now I'm sitting in the back of the classroom
pretending this is a bus

Where gonna role play the 1960s today, students!
Ya'll head to the front.
'Cause guess what?
You're better than us.

first,
I'd ask one of the jocks
to write me a paper on where
Kobe Bryant, Barry Bonds and Michael Vick
each messed up

Cause if you're as good as they say you are
and are smart enough to pay the extra money
to get an accountant you can trust
these papers will be far more educational
than one plus one.

I'd tell'em
life is more than a game
and for extra credit

I'd ask any black athlete in the class
to give me a comparative analysis
on the similarities 'tween pro ball and slavery

second,
I'd ask the Lair kid
why PlayStation 3's bomb,
will never be Dungeons and Dragons
why online gaming is cool
but it's important to have human interaction
and why he's so glad he has it with that
because his parents never had it with him

I want a speech about how you're gonna play
these games with your kid. Matter a' fact
make it a poem.

we got AYP and NCLB standards to meet
so I'd rather let your English teach 'til the test
while I test the teachers
or else they gon' close the doors to this lil' recess
and we're all going home

third,
I'd give'em all homework

At lunch, sit with a different race, gender, sexual preference
religion, physically handicapped or mental condition.
Starting with the role playing gamer and the jock…

You, Band Camp.

You, gangsta
and you, the punk.

'cause you can segregate into college prep and LD in here
but out there
there's strength in numbers.

I want papers about how every day
is another opportunity to educate
yourself or someone else
'cause some of us used to not be allowed
in these four walls to get this
and now some of us can't get it
'cause another four walls won't let us out

but get this
these four walls could be the biggest obstacle to you
'cause the real classroom
has a ceiling of clouds
and sometimes it has walls of injustice
and windows of misperception
but it's got a ground

and you've got two feet
so you can always walk,
wheel or fly your way to another lesson.

and that's what they taught me:
that no matter how much my pride wanted that self-serving
feel good, Michelle Pfeiffer, *Dangerous Minds* kind
of conviction
that noble sacrifice of a profession

I was no teacher

I was just a lesson

can't even call myself a good learner
but I learn
have learned and still do
but now
the classrooms are different

THE ART OF WAR

I did not kick or scream the day they relieved me of my post
the museum of handmade artwork
hung shivering on the meat locker walls of the hallway
gasped at me
like I was the one being lynched
stared at me
like my very short peers
as I took my last long walk

we are the same peaces
the artwork and the artist
cut from funding like an eccentric piece of fruit
unplugged, bitten
then left in a world to rot
never expecting piece
to bite back

but your Tree of Knowledge
Good and Evil
lives to bear fruit
withers without it
deflates like an empty wing
hollows like the echoes of children
long after they've flown the coup
forbid us from ourselves
and we are driven batty like barren mothers
who would murder for the possibility of creation

day six
you excommunicate us from your classrooms
because we are not your trinity
of science, math and history

we are the intersection
crucified on your standardized "X"
when all faith really is
is imagination

you make lamb out of your flock
sentence them to seven deadly periods
and a hot lunch
then hail me a heretic
they crucified your Jesus for being eccentric

fired women who practiced their craft
bludgeoned and belittled us with sticks and rocks
benchmarks and core curriculum
then had the nerve to call us stoners
your Atom
a pottery class
all Big Bang ashes
and dust and mud
your math
just a dance by the numbers
your history
a Pollock
depending upon which way you look at it
and who's looking

the day they killed my class
by castrating their leader
began a revolt of pent-up, pitch-forked aggression
because taking away how our kids feed their souls
is akin to taking away how we feed our families

disciplinary actions went up like walls around them
attendance and achievement
went down like self-esteem
on adolescent boys
all head
no heart

the day my school stopped educating the whole child
and let technology create our God
was the day my students picked up arms

that same hallway
still faintly wearing the scent of my perfume
the refrigerated walls still trying to contain the fire
in their stomach, mind and eyes

those same project portraits, wrinkled
bearing the age spots of appreciation
knowing they'll never be swapped out
because program funding ended months ago
with my job

reminders of an age more Romantic
a country more sophisticated
where hypertension and suicides are down
and average life expectancy and
erectile dysfunction are up!

my soldiers implemented our exit strategy
armed to the teeth with poetry and paint guns
strapped with pellets the size and color of the red pill
they bombed murals all over the superintendent's office

and her matching car
with a gradient the color of the sky on Creation Monday

day one
the day they relieved me of my post
for conduct not befitting a teacher
was the day after Columbine
this prank still a paper idea in my journal
thousands of miles away
right after water cooler drunk principal
budget cuts me in the throat and says

"We need more arts programs like we need a hole in the
    head!"

had I had a gun
instead of an outlet
I would have agreed.

CHILDREN OF THE SUNDAY

The difference between sunbathing
and bathing without water is subtle

a few degrees of separation when it's a hundred and four
you're a hundred and four
and the National Weather Service
won't turn the community center into shelter
until it's 105

like home and homeless, subtle
as the six degree separation in the air-conditioned
window of a heat advisory
we've been here all along
standing outside for a very long time
people of scorched earth and plenty

we do not tan, we burn
skin toned
palette of hues
gradient colors of a dancing flame
the only rainbow we're allowed
without water, just sun

in the absence of white sand,
called children of the dirt
star-front property by night
gaze into a sea of mountain from lawn chairs
perched in grassless yards by day
this pyramid a mesa makes

this city elevates us
serves us like a shoulder and white linen

to bronzed sun gods far from shorelines and vacations
this is our Gladiatorial Sacrifice

where we enjoy salt and see
people of prayers and pilgrimages
where water, itself, is a miracle
however, much more often, here
many a'miracle walk on without it

800 miles from Long Beach,
1400 miles from Tenochtitlan
baptized by both
blessed to be here

WORK

OF ANGELS AND SWEATSHOPS

The cure for poverty
is providing
I kid
that his kitten of a body
curled up
in the bonnet
of brand new sheets
purrs
like the bus pass we have
and the car
we do not
warm
like electric blankets
instead of
unpaid gas bills
he is a four year-old gift
gently used
hand me up
oblivious to all gift wrap
and bows
we cannot afford
the tissue paper
we've used to quicker-picker-upper
spills and tears
he hovers above the cracks
in this sidewalk
of a system

thanks to
Grandma and Grandpa Claus
because bikes
cannot be put on EBT cards

we cannot SNAP our way
out of this Black Magic, baby

he sleeps
oblivious
to the fact
that he is serenely
slumbering his way into a crater
deflation
sinking into this air mattress
our sheets aren't fitted for
the Sleep Number

we couldn't afford
unaware
of the fact that he sleeps on wings
that I've plucked from my back
feather by feather
that angels are manufactured in sweatshops
daily
that every pluck
sounds like the punch of a time clock
son,
I will give you a quill
everyday until I have no more to give
I will deposit them in your spine
until I am no longer wealthy with wings
in hopes
that you will
one day
right with one.

WORK

I

There are few things more difficult
than getting lipstick
out of a blue collar
for a few things
we work

work like
lipstick on a blue collar
like three jobs
and the sex
we still can't afford
to have
like a sex worker

fancy feet fantasies
of strawberry toes
dipped in fondue faces
while we rest
in the heel of society

I will never
let him have my feet
of running
kicking
and standing
instead of lying down

II

That pill
drug skid marks
down my esophagus
after kicking
and screaming
'cross my tongue

awoke
took my longest finger
out of me
at 6 o'clock

erected it
to twelve
and shoved it past
his sleeping nose

there is nothing sexy
about eye sockets.

when the perpetrator
sleeps over
it's date rape
whether the patron
paid
or not

III

my arms
are longer than his sentence
rivet strong and smooth

sometimes
for fastening
the maturation of
baby boys
to Maybe Men

other times
for the quickening
of the removal
of his sternum
from my bosom

maybe baby
maybe not
these arms
do not belong to him
they are open
to me

IV

My ankles
were pregnant
with desperate housework
when I collared him

lipstick I did not recognize
perfume I did

but did not blame her for being a victim
did not blame my hands
for refusing to wash
anymore of his fucking shirts

did not blame god
for leaving my daughter's father
and his patriarchal paycheck

for putting my baby girl
on my back
putting food and shelter
on my shoulders
making my living
off my ass

my brain
cannot be judged by its cover,
my complexion, nor my circumstance
not where I clock in
or clock out

I have a degree
in sociology
and survival
and only one
is coming in handy

V

My daughter
is my body of labor
a woman now
born from my rib
pushed from my pelvis
apple of my Eve
I named her "Eden"

she has nested with serpents
seen me
serve leg, thigh and breast
to a tapeworm society
that cannibalizes its women

she's seen
my serviceable body parts
removed
used to fill their holes
she's seen my heart overlooked
cast plate-side
like a gizzard
she's seen them
eat me
from the inside
out

VI

she barely remembers
my housewife days
of not lifting a finger
to her father

and him
putting himself
where ever he wanted
his fists
as hard as he wanted

and I chose
bait instead of bitch
I chose pussy
instead of prison
because I rather teach her

teach her
that there is dirt
underneath every French manicure
that working girls
get their ass kicked for a living

that's a choice for some
less of a choice for others
but so is getting your ass kicked
for love
for life

teach her

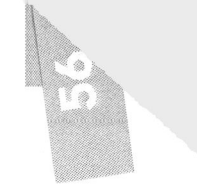

the difference between sale and sacrifice
is the cost and the price
like the difference between
pay equity and fair wage

teach her the difference between
high risk career
and poor life choices
that either way we have rights
even when they put their palms
over our voices

I taught her that
I'd rather give the street
what her father repeatedly took
even pride

what she learned from me
is the value of her body
for better or for worse

she learned not to stay for bullshit
like "relationships take work"
work takes work
and work consists
of whatever a body
is obliged to do.

CUBA, NM

At not a day over 7
maybe 8
she stood in between the double doors
on display

"Rest Stop"
wrong phrase to use
'cause she was definitely working
the absent smile was proof

not selling herself
but rather entire generations
picked, pushed, promised
then pulverized
into precious gems

worth more when rare
this was her culture
and as she has learned thus far
it is the one thing she can sell
better than them
the soul she can sell faster
than they sold theirs

one thing that they cannot take
only buy

no telling how long
she'd been standing there
before she unreturned my smile
barely pierced herself,
she hustles ear rings

that are not for ceremony
just tradition

holds them in arms that say "buy"
but stares at me with eyes that say "go away"
I could tell she'd been standing there
almost as long as we've been living here
from the burden of her gait

as she drug herself back
to mom's four door office
cell phone attached to mother's ear
in lieu of product she doesn't sniff
just like a pimp

burnin' minutes
baby girl hasn't worked
enough hours to prepay yet
but will

and I've seen us sell each other
in different forums
shrink rap ourselves
up into marketable art forms
but at least

for at least 7
maybe 8
hours on her feet
she put in an honest day's work to sell hers.

RUIDOSA, TX

They used to hold Mass
in three languages
in this town
300 people ago

before Candelaria
pirated our religion up river
back when Ruidosa
meant loud as the Rio Grande
when the border was
deaf, dumb and blind

back when the river
connected us for miles
instead of separating us by generations

tucked behind
the toothy smile
of the Chinati Mountains
this town sits
swallowed
in the valley of her gut

land that's been contested
since the Apaches and Jumanos
to today's cartels
on both sides of the border
and Congress
on both sides of the aisle

a town
that's been fought over

and fought for
now forgotten

75 miles
down the road
in Lajitas
tourists pay $800 a night
to stay at a resort

a town first known
for electing
a beer-drinking goat as its mayor

Ruidosa
now a town of only 19
is best known
for people electing
to leave

two businesses
and a church
all that is left
in a town known for
"getting by"
in so many ways

Ms. Celia Hill
the 82 year-old owner
of the La Junta General Store,
which neighbors the church,
has watched the adobe
evaporate for years

Mr. Blumberg
owns the other business in town
Ruidosa Cantina
for when both
the desert
and the Sacred Heart Mission Church
are drier than usual

a rancher as well
68 year-old Jim Blumberg
also owns
the only other lifestyle in town

a town where
cowboys and vaqueros
belly up to the bar together
like they piss in the same river
but nobody goes to church anymore

there is a temporary chapel
in the adobe building
adjacent the church
that has a roof,
unlike the Sacred Heart,
now sunbathing its altar

in a reminder
of the sacrifices
made to the sun god
each day
in this region

where Franciscans
built missions
to bring Christianity
to those crossing the border
at Presidio

where the Mexican government
established a penal colony
and assembled armed convicts
against the Comanches

where Pancho Villa
let the revolution rest,
regroup
and ride onto our blank canvas

resistance
like the graffiti
now adorning the well-worn walls of the church
as sacrilegious and sacred as its namesake

they herd artists here now
right up the road in Marfa
towns can't afford to move
towns have to switch careers too
in order to survive

but I wouldn't call it a ghost town
not while the church
still has walls
pressed together like hands

crumbling
but still praying
like people

nah,
I wouldn't call it ghost town
not while it's still got soul.

AS AMERICAN AS APPLESEED

The questions consume us
land stewardship versus
organic food stores
skin or real estate
the state question

an official designation
federally recognized
certified "our planet"
WE ARE ORGANIC
people of red meat
flesh and bone

not modern
nothing new
under the sun
children of the seed
protecting the genes
refusing to be
Government Modified Organisms

blood quantum by the bottle
label out sides
when insides aren't known
there is no seal
that makes us New Mexican
not even a fraction of us
is synthetic

there are those
that farm our culture
from our food

their questions
consume us

we do not pray in red or green
only blessings
as we feast
on good and evil apple trees
Rome Beauty in Embudo
Champagne in Dixon
apples to apples
dust to dust

LETTER TO
HIP HOP

SILENT SANCTUARY

The poet entered the sanctuary
as a cynic not a sinner
a seer
not a sayer
this time

this time
he was looking
for the word

this time
he needed inspiration
more than he needed
to be inspiring

and he was listening
for once
maybe twice

the poet entered the sanctuary
as a sentencer
but not like them
not a judge
but one who strings words
into rosaries
that protect us
from not talking to each other
that shackle us to communities
for life

the poet entered the sanctuary

stood in the doorway of silence
praying to be met with
music, mantra, melody
even magic

he was met with none
as he crossed the threshold
between craft and creation
as he has learned
on the street

that science ain't shit
without sanctity
that anyone can read the notes
it's how you play'em
anyone can write and read a word
it's how you lay'em
how you say'em
anyone can read a holy book
it's how you live it
people sleep under sheet music
all the time
and don't give a fuck
it's how you make love

the poet entered the sanctuary
to have his French pardoned
amongst other things
but was disappointed
because there would be more French

disappointed

that God's people
were worshipping with mouths closed

disappointed
that God's people
were worshipping with asses still

disappointed
that heavenly people
were afraid to love one another
to touch one another
to dance

confused
that they could read
a whole book
and have nothing to say
that they could read
an entire hymnal
and have nothing to sing
nothing to dance

who could read
an entire volume
of divine poetry
and then pray in silence?

so the poet left the sanctuary
back to the curbside pulpit
where pain
and worship
both have to be louder than the traffic

where God is a superhero
and you only ever see her
when your life's in danger
and unlike the church folk
'cause of the nature of how he lives
he sees God everyday
doesn't even have to pray

but when he does
when they do
they have a novel on the tip of their tongues

and God likes stories
a lot

but the poet forgot
that their poetry
comes from silence
not from sounds

and such poetry
if it's good
leads back
to silence
again

amen.

GENERATION

My Generation is turnin' the big three-oh
but we don't say the T-word though

grew up to not be monsters
though we still get treated like toddlers
and though not much was expected out of us
we've surprised ourselves

we've got no 60s remedies
no 70s memories to "un"remember
'cause drugs were that good
back when sex was that safe

we're 80s babies
born out of a fear of anything
that brings happiness
from backpack gangsta rap to the AIDS plague

born after a generation that
legalized it for commercial drug slangers
rapped our wrist with rulers' English
even spellchecked our bible papers
stole our recreation and called it escapism
we're criminal but they're innocent

turned youthful indiscretion
into these mandatory sentences
that same generation
with that age-old story about
"not having any capable off-spring
to take over the family business"
said we have no experiences

left us no shoes to fill in
'cause they been barefooted in hippie kitchens
since back when they was still pregnant with us
and even though they wood stock-piled up
an inexhaustible amount of outdated references
I gotta say

if they would have made the world perfect
like they said they would
they wouldn't be fed up with us
for not filling the position they left open
with the 40 year-old job description

but it's not about them
or what kind of mess was left for us
or even what's expected of us
it's what we've accomplished
the generation that turned Saving-the-World Inc.
into non-profits

the folk music of our generation
was first played with Texas Instruments
the kids who used to spend 8 hours a day
solitary confinement with their Sega Genesis
turned into adults who can't put a straight
8-hour workday of productivity together
without sneakin' a peak at their social network
but at least we got friends in different countries yo!

got cadets in barracks playin' FIFA '09
with cats in Iraq all night long

we're the generation that got passed homogenous
we got post-modern

white parents raised on Save the Last Dance
wanna put they kids in a hip hop class
and the wave of second generation,
suburban Black parents
send their youth to spend summers
schooling with relatives still inner city
learning how to read the streets

so we don't forget the ABCs of poverty
we're the generation that evolved
from just having gay "friends"
to queer relatives and same sex partners
we've domesticated men and turned women into ballers

we got hip hoppers rockin' mohawks
battlin' punk rock over who's got the skinniest jeans
Big and Rich
even country done gone corporate
spinnin' rims replace pairs of horses
'cause you can't put butterfly doors on them things

but with all our faults
we're changin'
learnin' from our children,

instead of just sayin' what they ain't
'cause if there's one thing we did learn
from the Boomers it's how to make babies
despite the common "boogey man"-ing growin' up

"Sexual activity leads to arthritis and rabies."

they taught us about peace and love life
and we ran away with it

too old to be delinquent
too three-oh to abscond
bags packed with pride, indignation
and a healthy critique of everything
except ourselves

my generation of opinionated mumblers
and articulate apathy
are very vocal about what we don't care for
but extremely active for what we do

and sometimes
when we are not being chastised for speaking up
nor implored to shut up
we have our own battles to paci-fight
freak flags to wave
much to do and mouthful more to say
for ourselves

and many more years to prove it at only three-oh
but one thing we won't do
is we won't say the T-word though

LETTER TO HIP HOP I

Dear Hip Hop
open your speakers
so you can speak "us"
hear us

mirrors
we are what you look like
in the morning
good morning
from the kids you never slept on

chased Boogie Monsters out of our imagination
through headphones
the ones I snuck
under sheet music
when mom banished the TV from my bedroom

from the generation that considered silence
violence
you lullabyed us
pops worked two jobs so I could buy you

and I knew
when I grew up
I wanted to be just like you
the bastard love child of Gospel and Rock
you are what Blues turned into
just to get hitchhikers to pick her up

a wax museum of classic sculptures
that never so much as flinched
when they called you "vulture"

you're the swan song of ugly ducklings

with your puberty of percussion
you turned awkward into popular
for many an acned b-girl
and four-eyed beat boxer

for all the kids
who couldn't play
football, basketball or soccer

the same kids who
stayed up all night
playing Halo
and make believe movies of mobsters

but your competition's a little more honest
two heartless sleeves in a steel cage match
soul, saliva and spit
sprawled across the celebrity death rap

we fight the way you taught us
in the absence of battered mothers
and abusive fathers
we became deadbeat authors
break beat martyrs

the music of your generation
resurrected in HI-DEFinition audio

Dear Hip-Hop
we bomb these letters

upside the womb of your Manhattan Projects
we are your Trinity products
however, nonviolent
the kids who are still feeling you
in Hiroshima and Nagasaki

LETTER TO HIP HOP II

Dear Hip-Hop
when no one listened to us
you spoke "us"
like Huffy bicycles
and E.T. childhoods

around blocks
you'd ride us
before tricked-out cars
and handle bars
you read us bedtime stories
while our parents argued

before you were profiled
on America's Most Harmful
you were most wanted
on our Christmas lists

the secret we shared with our best friends
gone public
when they branded you "thuggish"
but we still loved you
we recognized family members
by iTunes playlists and Timbs

different shades of kin
not so much recognized by our skin
but rather the songs that we sing

you might call them hymns
and we might call you the resurrection
eulogy to the life we once lived

the new career that didn't exist
more than a way to feed our kids

you are the borrowed wings
that we've used to raise them
the heartbeats we gave them to play with
the sandbox we freestyled to William & Kate them
Queens and Latin King them

as a parent in a broke beat generation
you taught us how to four finger ring them

so we bring you
this offering of thanks
from your offspring
who never made enough
to afford you a respectable
Father's Day gift

instead
we learned to serve the community you left
our Juneteenth of breath

a bunch of poor kids
from the wrong side
of the Cross Bronx Expressway
with nothing to do

but this.

LETTER TO HIP HOP III

Dear Hip-Hop
we write these letters with bubbles
with slanguage you've given us
the Queen's English we never gave a shit about
we write you this in her severed tongue
we refund

so we give back
to you
to what once was a community
before it became a music

before you were newsless
the CNN of the hood
now reminds me of the Jersey Shore

yes,
I actually grew up there

back when it was a real place
like you
not a fairy tale
or fantasy

when reality
was a flow
and not a show
before it was about "show"
when it was about substance
when it was about funk
about Fresh

about us
not about them

wasn't allowed to meet you
til my parents let me
at seven
and I been spending my allowance
on you ever since
you give courage to cowardly kids
we now call "swagger"

you are the first date break up music
a bastard's Father's Day anthem
the lone ring tone on that single mother's phone
she calls it sanity
she calls you sanity

so we give thanks for your candor
you remind us that that the world is ours
if we ask for it

JAMESETTA

The day you died, God
stopped questioning
his son's sexuality

33-year-old Nazarene
with no kids
at a time when
men fathered at 19
and grandfathered at 38

no Mary Magdalene
no Mary Kate and Ashley
no Mary Jane

yes,
there were questions
in heaven
bigger than
does it exist?
and it does.

there was living proof
every time you opened your mouth, Etta

like a Black Sabbath
you had a voice that would…
that would make God
rest on the seventh day

just like God
patting himself
on the back

at the sound of you
we admire
stare at you
like our own

like our own reflections
spidered in the mirror
hungover
because our Sunday Kinda Love
didn't make it past Saturday night
fractured

leaving us with questions
questions like
"Why can't I sing like that!?"
and "I thought she was in recovery?"
questions like
"Why does it seem like
the most broken lives
give us the most solid voices?"

the most complete
most whole
most holy voices
Jamesetta Hawkins
a name only a teenage mother could love
and she did

you and Jesus
had more in common
than single mothers
and invisible fathers

called your mom
"The Mystery Lady"
and imagine
they pro'lly thought
the same thing
about Virgin de Guadalupe
and her kid
with the immaculate childhood
a different kind of prodigy

had you turned around
and split
like your name

Etta James
is who you was
after you went blonde
after you were told
to take advantage
of your light complexion

after you agreed
to dye everything
except your eyebrows
'cause you wanted to
look like a "bad girl"

you bad girl!
bad enough to
make B.B. King
sweet on you

at 16
in addiction recovery by 21

gone 5 days
before your 74th
dementia
but still telling
anyone who cares to listen
that you remember

that when you were still a child
people used to travel miles
just to hear you sing
perform your own kind of miracles
in temples
with money changers and prostitutes
a prodigy too

with a voice
as milk and honey
as the heaven you're from
no wonder
we're still addicted to what you sung
it comes from heroin in ya lungs

been going thru withdrawals
since you've been gone, now

I'm the one with the weight problem
waiting for your next album
fiending without you
'cause we can't hear you sing anymore

celestial body
long before Hollywood's
Walk of Fame
gave you a star

we weren't prepared
for your hour-glass frame
to break
leaving Sugar All Over our floors
you said you
"sang the songs that people needed to hear"

and Jesus?
was half "people"
and God was disturbed
that his son kept a diary
however,
God was damn happy
that his very good looking
but very single son
wrote this
about you, Etta
in his diary

"You sang,
You sang.
Oh and then the spell was cast
and here we are now in heaven.
For you are mine
at last."

and that
was the day
the angels
got their voice back.

IMMORTAL TECHNIQUE

He raised his hand
said he didn't understand
    why rap artist Immortal Technique was so angry.
I thought about questions asked of me before,
then questions began looking like answers
like

why do the inner city kids ice grill instead of grin
as though all their problems can be solved
by an "enwhitened" household and positive thinking
not by correcting the socioeconomic status
of oppressed people
instead of corrections of oppressed people

jobs three times less likely to hire black males than whites
that's just McDonald's and Footlocker
those who ask these questions would feel
a sense of accomplishment
by giving an urban youth the chance to rock those zebra stripes
"In a store full of icy white Nikes,
surely you can find some bootstraps to pull yourself up by"
on a dying wage that most kids would rather die than get paid
same question asker had the audacity to say
"Hey, why y'all kill each other over sneakers anyway?"

maybe because back in the day
    y'all wouldn't let us wear anything but soft shoe
cause Mark Twain is such a "great American writer"
    that Huckleberry Finn is both
a tragedy to me and a comedy to you
but mandatory reading for everyone in junior high school
as horrific an institution as slavery.

"Oh they were just products of their generation..."
well then *this* is a just product of our generation
gangster repertory instruction in our multicultural classrooms
full of colorful language but lacking truth
lesson plan some Goodfellas, Scarface and Gangs of New York
to teach them about immigrants
Plymouth Rock genocides
    and John Smith forcing himself on an underage papoose

while we're scaring them to death in the school house
    with textbooks that actually have a spine
show them nine dead during the holiday shopping season
Omaha, Nebraska cornhusker eating white guy
just like you, teacher
teach the kids what it will do to their dreams
    when it only seems to be them
    they see on the nightly news
imagine the nightmares they have for homework every night
and the extra credit?

is waking up to a nightmare too
but they should just be happy to be alive, right?
they ice grill stoic and animate frowns
because the lower they're oppressed, the more they're "down"
frankly, we've been made to coon smile so long
the atrophied muscles in our blackface don't work
so well now, boss!

so check an Aunt Jemimah bottle or an Uncle Ben's Rice
the answer was in his question when he asked,

"Well, then why do black people spend
their whole life savings on ice?"
maybe because you make us
believe worth is acquired
not God-given
community below competition
we want to be what we see on television
white lines, blue eyes, hair we can lie, dye and buy
our citizenship
the answer my friend
is changing the "why" to I
we can either lie or die but don't "bi"
this bullshit-ass citizenship
we were three-fifths,
the 40 acres and a mule was a myth
so some of us decided to get the other two-for-five with white
    rocks to be whole in the eyes of the world
iced outside
    so inside we're getting sick
so instead of building houses
we are just flipping bricks
or should I just have just said it was Willie Lynch?

when you are accustomed to being enslaved
someone can unlock the shackles on your legs,
but not in your brain
so instead of running away, you find a way
to get'em custom fitted
then I imagine him asking...
"Why do you hate the white man?"
    I want to say "Nah man, that ain't it..."
but for years

we weren't allowed to do anything but love him
under penalty of death
so when you push the pendulum so far to the white is right,
it is going to swing back til all that's pro-black is left!

but you should be asking questions like
"Why don't the blacks fight back,
kill us in equal numbers for all the years we killed them?"
It's because my people are evolved contrary to eugenics
though centuries of war on our vessel
have shell-shocked us on a sometimes wayward direction,
we remain as moral a compass as those old negro spirituals
at our center
so, the answer is not as passive-aggressive
as racist questions like
"Can't you write a poem about anything other than race?"
I say sure, as soon as race doesn't matter
and the fact that he even raised his hand to ask
a question like that
well, therein lies the answer
until we realize the role we played
in Technique's anger
we will never understand him
or America
or ourselves.

so I quote:
Throw your hands in the air
and wave 'em like you just don't...

... care

MEMORIAL

It's quieter when people fall
skin and knees don't sound like a cabinet full
of kitchen pots when they hit the floor
it's different

quieter
not as much racket
blood leaks quietly unlike faucets

but when graven images collapse
when statues shatter
concrete and medal
it is loud and messy
they don't heal
or put themselves back together like us

but then again
they were never like us in the first place

cement boots don't allow
a lot of room for movement
when a sculpture's position changes
it is usually from erect
to down

people give
and take
only break when doing too much of one
or the other

one day
we'll build people out of icons

instead of building statues out of busted people

grounds keeping
'cause we should at least treat each other
as well as we treat our memories
treat each other like we'll be here
for the next hundred years
treat us larger than life

because we look just like heroes
and act like them, too

when we move.

EDWARD HAKIM BELLAMY

became the inaugural poet laureate of Albuquerque on April 14th, 2012, at age 33. He was the son of a preacher man (and a praying woman). His mother gave him his first book of poetry as a teen, a volume by Khalil Gibran.

Many poems later, Bellamy has been on two national champion poetry slam teams, won collegiate and city poetry slam championships (in Albuquerque and Silver City, NM), and has been published in numerous anthologies and on inner-city buses. A musician, actor, journalist, playwright and community organizer, Bellamy has also received an honorable mention for the Paul Bartlett Ré Peace Prize at the University of New Mexico. Bellamy is the founder and president of Beyond Poetry LLC. For more information on the author, please visit www.hakimbe.com.